W0081826

The
Nothing to Fear
JOURNAL

The
Nothing
to Fear
JOURNAL

Questions and Reflections for
Demystifying and Preparing
for the End of Life

Julie McFadden, RN

Tarcher
an imprint of Penguin Random House
New York

Tarcher
an imprint of Penguin Random House LLC
1745 Broadway, New York, NY 10019
penguinrandomhouse.com

Copyright © 2025 by Julie McFadden
Penguin Random House values and supports copyright. Copyright fuels creativity, encourages diverse voices, promotes free speech, and creates a vibrant culture. Thank you for buying an authorized edition of this book and for complying with copyright laws by not reproducing, scanning, or distributing any part of it in any form without permission. You are supporting writers and allowing Penguin Random House to continue to publish books for every reader. Please note that no part of this book may be used or reproduced in any manner for the purpose of training artificial intelligence technologies or systems.

Tarcher is a registered trademark of Penguin Random House LLC, and Tarcher with leaf design is a trademark of Penguin Random House LLC

Most Tarcher books are available at a discount when purchased in quantity for sales promotions or corporate use. Special editions, which include personalized covers, excerpts, and corporate imprints, can be created when purchased in large quantities. For more information, please e-mail specialmarkets@penguinrandomhouse.com. Your local bookstore can also assist with discounted bulk purchases using the Penguin Random House corporate Business-to-Business program. For assistance in locating a participating retailer, e-mail B2B@penguinrandomhouse.com.

Book design by Shannon Nicole Plunkett

Trade Paperback ISBN: 9780593855256
Ebook ISBN: 9780593855263

Printed in the United States of America
1st Printing

The authorized representative in the EU for product safety and compliance is Penguin Random House Ireland, Morrison Chambers, 32 Nassau Street, Dublin D02 YH68, Ireland, https://eu-contact.penguin.ie.

Contents

Introduction — *vii*

Part 1

Becoming More Comfortable
with the End of Life — 1

Part 2

Advice for the Dying — 23

Part 3

Advice for Caregivers — 67

Part 4

Practical Considerations — 121

Final Note — *147*

Introduction

In my recent book, *Nothing to Fear*, I describe my experiences as a hospice nurse. I've witnessed so many amazing, beautiful, and even miraculous things. I've been with dying people whose eyes fill with wonder as they tell me they see angels or hear music; others' faces light up with smiles. Often, it is just the simple beauty of the body taking care of itself. The most miraculous things that I see are the families—the love shared between patients and their families in the moments leading up to death. People who send me messages frequently assume being a hospice nurse is depressing and that witnessing death is sad and terrible, but in so many ways, I find that it's actually the opposite! I get to witness so much love and serve another human being during such a vulnerable time at the end of their life. It's an incredible and sacred gift.

When people are willing to discuss the end of their lives and accept that they're going to die, their whole being changes. They seem to carry with them a special kind of freedom, an attitude that truly helps them live their last days. Their fear decreases, they feel freer, and, ironically, they actually seem more full of life, even though they're dying.

I think this change in perspective can apply to *all* people because, technically, we're all dying. If we can face that fact and allow in a bit of that freedom, I believe we all can live better lives here and now.

In the pages that follow, you'll find information, prompts, and space to collect your thoughts and feelings on the end-of-life journey, whether your own or a loved one's. I encourage you to think and write openly, regardless of where you are in the journey. The space you're creating will help you and those closest to you be more present at the end of life—which is truly a gift.

Part 1

Becoming More Comfortable with the End of Life

If death is normalized and discussed often, we each can walk toward our final days with a lot less fear.

Part 1 of this journal is for anyone, whether you are caring for a loved one, facing your own end-of-life experience, or simply interested in the reality of the dying process, which we all will eventually face. Try not to censor yourself as you work through this book—write freely and see what comes up for you. There are no right or wrong answers.

Choosing Acceptance over Fear

My experience as a hospice nurse has shown me that people who are willing to be honest about their feelings relating to the end of life seem to find the most ease and peace. When you think about the end of life, what comes up? What scares you the most? Try not to hold back—write what comes to mind.

Think back to the passing of a loved one that felt peaceful and filled with love and care. What went smoothly?

How were you able to be present for this person as the end of their life approached?

How were others present, either physically or otherwise, and caring?

Are there things you would change about the experience, even though there are things that went well?

Now think back to the passing of a loved one that did not feel peaceful or filled with love and care. What was missing?

Who, if anyone, provided emotional support and patient advocacy for the dying person?

What would you do differently if you could?

Looking back over your responses to the peaceful and not-peaceful passings of loved ones, what stands out to you most? What, in your experience, are the ingredients for a peaceful death? What would the setting be? Who would be present? What emotions and conversations would you most want to have? We'll explore these ideas in more depth later; for now, simply write what comes to mind.

When facing a terminal diagnosis, whether for yourself or a loved one, it's tempting to hold on to hope for good news, even after it is no longer realistic to do so. During my years as an intensive care unit (ICU) nurse, I saw this scenario play out among families all too often.

Paradoxically, there is a freedom and peace that can come with facing reality instead of denying it.

In other aspects of life, have you experienced the freedom of acceptance rather than avoiding a difficult truth? Describe how it felt—both before and after that moment of acceptance.

In thinking about the end of life, what aspects of the experience make you want to retreat the most? What are your go-to ways to deny or escape the reality of the situation?

What are some ways you can begin to acknowledge and accept the reality as an end-of-life journey unfolds, to begin to feel more peace and less fear, for yourself and your loved one(s)?

As a hospice nurse, I know firsthand that there are outcomes worse than the end of life. Physical pain and discomfort, miscommunication, confusion, and unrealistic hopes are all unnecessary forms of suffering. What comes to mind when you think about outcomes that are worse than the end of life?

Death Is Not a Dirty Word

In my work with the dying, I see over and over again how many of us are afraid to talk about the end of life. The more comfortable we are talking about death, the better we'll live, and the better we'll die.

Use the chart below to list ways we avoid talking about death—and some clearer, more honest alternatives.

COMMON PHRASE	CLEARER ALTERNATIVE
"She's gone."	"She has died."
"He won't be with us much longer."	"He's dying."

It can be challenging to start a conversation with loved ones about the end of life. Often, however, others are willing to discuss it once you begin the dialogue. What are some ways you could bring up the topic with trusted family and friends? Having an opening line ready can help create a welcoming space for sharing—for example, bringing up this journal in conversation can be a starting point that creates a safe space for an honest talk.

PERSON IN MY LIFE	POSSIBLE OPENING SENTENCE(S) TO START A CONVERSATION

Envisioning a Peaceful Death

I think it's important to talk about death with the person who is dying when they're lucid. I see that it helps my patients, and their loved ones, to talk about their death ahead of time. I'll often begin, "We all have an end-of-life journey. Right now, yours is a little clearer than other people's. What's that going to look like? How do you want to live the rest of your days?" Use the space below to write your answer.

(Some suggestions of things they could think about: Do they have an idea of when they would want to stop treatment? Would they want to be home with family and friends caring for them?)

Permission Granted

Many people feel they have to use every means necessary, for as long as possible, to keep themselves or a loved one alive. But I want to give you permission to allow the dying process to happen. Below, write a permission note to yourself or a loved one. Lovingly say that it's okay to let go.

Dear _____,

Dear _____,

Journaling

As many of my social media followers know, I've been journaling on and off for the past twenty years. This practice has shaped the way I view myself and the world around me, and it has given me great relief during challenging times. You should journal in any way you feel comfortable, but if you have no idea where to start, here's how I do it.

I begin by directly addressing my higher power, who I choose to call God because that's what's easiest for me. You don't have to use *God*; the point is to write to someone or something you feel connected to, like the universe or nature, or for caregivers, the loved one you're caring for or grieving.

Then I write down everything, absolutely everything, in my heart and mind: the good, the bad, and the ugly. Sometimes, I'm writing so fast that it's barely legible. That's okay. I don't hide anything. It's a way of getting out everything that's inside me, emptying me onto the page. For me, it releases the grief.

Over the years, especially during my most desperate times, I believe I've heard back from God (or the universe or whoever). I've had many days when I was writing about my grief and felt I was receiving a beautiful message of love and support in response. This doesn't always happen, of course, and it's not why I journal, but when it does, it's a lovely benefit.

As you make your way through this guided journal, I encourage you to write freely. If needed, continue your thoughts in a separate notebook or journal. If it feels right, continue the practice over time, after you've finished this book. In my experience, the time and effort will pay off in many, and unexpected, ways.

Part 2

Advice for the Dying

If you know how you want to die, it will help you decide, with the time you have left, how you want to live.

So many things in life are beyond our control. If you are faced with a terminal diagnosis, I encourage you to choose, as much as possible, how you want your journey to unfold. In this part, you'll find ways to embrace the gifts that a prepared death can give you.

Checklist for an Intentional End-of-Life Journey

☐ Do the self-growth work you want to do to accept your death—for example, working through this journal, trying simple meditation practices, or starting therapy to work through the things that have held you back.

☐ Tell your family and friends that you love them.

☐ Ask for forgiveness from the people you've hurt.

☐ Exercise healthy boundaries around your space, which might mean excluding people who may be harmful to you.

☐ Ask yourself what brings you the most joy and then do it.

Preparing for a Peaceful Death

I often ask patients, "What do you want these last months to look like? Do you want to be at home with your family? Do you want good pain management and symptom management? You don't have to make a choice today, but think about your responses. You get to decide." We'll get into more detail later, but for now, how would you respond?

Where I'd like to be:

People I would like to be present:

These next two items will help you think through how medicated you would like to be—for example, whether you would rather tolerate some pain in order to be more alert and awake—and will serve as a reminder about the things you can advocate for when the time comes.

Pain-management wishes:

Symptom-management wishes:

Accepting Help

You might feel the urge to resist the help family and friends offer you. I encourage you to open yourself to their help, and receive it with gratitude, as much as you can. What are your go-to ways of saying no? What could you say instead? It might be useful to remember that you're helping "your people" by letting them help you.

WAYS I REJECT HELP	WHAT I COULD SAY INSTEAD
Saying I'm too busy	I have plenty of food, but I could use a pair of warm socks . . .

Who is most likely to offer you help, and in what capacity? Can you envision a response that welcomes their help? And if they offer something you don't want, can you think of a way to suggest something you actually would find helpful—for example, suggesting breakfast instead of dinner, if that's what you really need?

Person in my life: _____

Help they are offering: _____

_____

Welcoming response: _____

_____

Person in my life: _____

Help they are offering: _____

_____

Welcoming response: _____

_____

Person in my life: _____

Help they are offering: _____

_____

Welcoming response: _____

_____

Person in my life: _____

Help they are offering: _____

_____

Welcoming response: _____

_____

Person in my life: _____

Help they are offering: _____

_____

Welcoming response: _____

_____

Person in my life: _____

Help they are offering: _____

_____

Welcoming response: _____

_____

Person in my life: _____

Help they are offering: _____

_____

Welcoming response: _____

_____

Person in my life: _____

Help they are offering: _____

_____

Welcoming response: _____

_____

How to Communicate with
Maximum Clarity

You can use this script as a guide for communicating with your doctor with maximum clarity:

Give permission. "I welcome you to speak candidly with me."

Ask about the likely progression. "I'm interested in knowing the likely progression and outcome of this disease."

Inquire about treatment options. "I'm interested to know if there are treatment options that have proven effective."

Ask about hospice. "I'd like to know if it would be better not to pursue treatments. Is there a point at which you may suggest hospice care?"

If your doctor still avoids the issue, you also could try asking, point blank, "If your mother had this, what would you recommend? If it were *you*, what would you do?"

Using Your Resources

If you are in hospice care, a number of people are at your disposal. Please take advantage of what they have to offer, and let them know what you need. Use the space below to jot notes about each type of caregiver. If you're not sure what resources are available to you, start with your doctor or hospice provider.

Hospice doctor:

Hospice nurse:

Hospice social worker:

Hospice chaplain:

Home health aide:

Volunteers:

Bereavement specialist:

Personal resources:

Family:

Friends:

Having Difficult Conversations

In my work as a hospice nurse, I've witnessed the power of end-of-life conversations with loved ones. It's common, and understandable, to want to avoid uncomfortable thoughts and feelings, but I encourage you to try to talk to your loved ones about what you're facing.

Who are you pushing away that you actually would like to let in?

How could you begin to reach out to them?

Discussing the reality of your situation can put others at ease. What can you envision saying to each loved one to open a dialogue and welcome them into your journey? Your statements might differ based on which person you're addressing.

Talking about Your Feelings

When we resist our feelings, they don't go away. When we embrace them, though, they lose their power to cause us suffering. Face your feelings—first by feeling them yourself and then by talking about them with others you love and trust. Not only does this create space for you, it can also make room for others to feel what they're feeling.

What I'm feeling:

What I can say to . . .

A partner:

A family member:

A dear friend:

A child:

What I can say to myself, or to a higher power (if applicable):

Talking about Dying

Be bold; talk about death. Most people don't want to, but when you push through your discomfort and fear, you'll find something extraordinary on the other side: peace. If your death has not yet been part of the conversation in your family or in your home, your loved ones might not know that it's okay to talk about it with you. Bring it up first, and when you do, don't sanitize it. Use all the d-words: *dying, death, dead, died.*

What are some d-word statements you can draft, with the goal of sharing them with your loved ones?

People often use phrases like "She passed away" or "He's gone to heaven," believing they are more comforting than discussing death in a more direct way. I find that simply saying "He's dying" can be more caring because it helps ease the fear and avoidance by addressing things head-on. Use the space below to explore the "comforting" phrases and what you might say instead.

"COMFORTING" PHRASE	DIRECT PHRASE

Talking about What's Unresolved (Maybe)

Are there relationships in your life that have unresolved problems? Do you need to make amends with anyone? Is there something you still need to say to someone? Consider talking about what's unresolved, if you sense there's a real possibility it will bring you or someone else freedom.

Person I could make amends with:

What's been left unsaid:

How I could begin the conversation:

Person I could make amends with:

What's been left unsaid:

How I could begin the conversation:

Person I could make amends with:

What's been left unsaid:

How I could begin the conversation:

How would starting these conversations bring peace to me and/or the other person? (If it would not, you aren't obligated to go there. The decision is yours.)

We can't expect someone who has never been emotionally mature to suddenly be able to discuss hard things. Use the space below for a conversation with yourself, or to write a letter you'll never send. This is about freeing *yourself* from a burden you're carrying.

Being Your Own Advocate

I always encourage patients and their loved ones to be educated advocates. This involves two steps. First, educate yourself. Research your disease, and know what to expect. Of course, you'll also be talking with your doctor. Use the space below to gather your key findings and conversation notes so you can reference them later.

The symptoms I can expect as my disease progresses are:

The specific care I may need or am concerned about is:

The second step in being an educated advocate is to speak up for your wishes. If your doctor doesn't bring up hospice care, you can bring it up yourself. Use the questions and space below to help manage this process. When in doubt, check it out: you can call a hospice company yourself and ask questions, even without a doctor's referral.

When you bring up hospice care, how does your doctor respond? Are they comfortable with the topic?

If the doctor is quick to dismiss your questions, saying "We're not there yet," envision your possible responses below.

Processing Difficult Emotions

Anticipatory grief is an emotional journey that both a terminally ill person and their loved ones embark on as they confront the impending loss. For yourself, in addition to managing physical symptoms, you are likely to experience an overwhelming range of emotions, including sadness, fear, anger, and anxiety. Paradoxically, creating space for these feelings can help you cope better—and can even lead to personal growth, acceptance, and finding peace within yourself. Use the space on the next few pages to unpack how you're feeling. This is an ongoing process that will change over time, and counseling or therapy also can help.

When I'm feeling deep sadness, what comes up most is:

When I'm feeling afraid, what comes up most is:

When I'm feeling anger, what comes up most is:

When I'm feeling anxious, what comes up most is:

When I think about transcending fear, what comes up most is:

When I think about spiritual exploration, what comes up most is:

When I think about peace, what comes up most is:

Contemplating Your Legacy

Reflecting on your life is a powerful part of preparing for death. It can be overwhelming, confusing, painful . . . and beautiful. What are you most proud of—not just achievements, but the legacy of love and connection that will live on after you're gone? Use the following pages to begin to collect your thoughts. Continue in another notebook or journal, or with the help of a professional, if needed.

What I'm most proud of:

How would I want to be remembered? Am I currently living and acting in the way I want to be remembered?

Things I would like to resolve, for more closure:

Is there anything I would change in my life? If so, how can I take steps to change these things, starting today?

Write a letter to a loved one, describing the legacy of love and care you are leaving them with. Whether you deliver this letter or not is up to you.

Dear _____,

Dear _____,

Part 3

Advice for Caregivers

The rules at the end of life are different from the rules at other stages of life because the goal has changed.

Taking care of someone at the end of their life is one of the greatest acts of love a person can perform. It is love in action—and a great deal of work. On the pages that follow, you'll find questions and suggestions focused not on the person who's dying, but instead focused on you. Yes, the practical aspect of your caregiving work matters, but it's also essential to take care of your own emotions during this challenging time. Most of all, I encourage you to be present during this beautiful, love-filled, and sacred time.

Letting Go of the Fighting Mentality

It's tempting to resist the reality of what's happening to your loved one. When we don't know what to say, and we're desperate for their health to be restored, we often go into "fighting mode." This is not helpful. Consider the following "fighting" personas and how you can shift your mindset to be more present for your loved one. (For more information on these personas, see chapter 8 in my first book, *Nothing to Fear*.)

The cheerleader:

What they say:

What you can say instead:

The religious one:

What they say:

What you can say instead:

The optimist:

What they say:

What you can say instead:

The denier:

What they say:

What you can say instead:

What thoughts and emotions does "giving up the fight" for your loved one's health bring up for you? How can you put aside these concerns to be more accepting of reality, both for their sake and for your own?

How can we redefine *hope* in this situation? It doesn't mean "They have to live forever"; instead, it could mean "My loved one laughs daily" or other meaningful goals in light of the reality they are facing. What could *hope* mean now?

Letting Your Loved One Be Your Guide

The more we let the dying person's body be the guide, the better they'll feel and the more peacefully they'll die. If their body wants to sleep, they should sleep. If they're not hungry, they don't have to eat. This, along with offering pain medications, might bring up feelings and concerns for you. Put them aside, and help make the patient's death as gentle as possible.

How does it feel to give up control of things like food, water, and medication and instead follow their body's needs? How can you work through your hesitations?

"Your loved one isn't dying because they aren't eating and drinking; they aren't eating and drinking because they are dying."

When your loved one is alert and oriented, they are the captain of the ship, and their wishes should be respected. What are they asking for?

How can you best honor their wishes?

When your loved one is no longer alert and oriented, pay close attention to what their body is saying. What messages are they sending, and how can you best respond? When in doubt, ask your hospice team to help you decipher the body's nonverbal communication.

How can you practice just "being" with your loved one, not constantly "doing" for them? If they are already **clean, safe, and comfortable** (see page 91), how can you be present in this moment together?

Don't Force It

It's tempting to want to impose your own vision and care agenda onto the person who is dying. Resist this urge. The process of dying requires letting go. Forced physical exertion, forced feeding, and forced hydration are *not* part of the hospice process. There are medical reasons not to force food or water—and most of all, the body knows what to do. Use the space below to reflect on your own inner struggle to honor the process.

Ways I'm tempted to give care:

What I can do instead:

Clearing the Bedside Table

When your loved one is approaching death and no longer eating or drinking, it can be time to clear away the snacks and drinks in their space, in both a literal and a metaphorical sense. What is the clutter, both physical and otherwise, that you can put aside to create space for acceptance and peace?

Physical clutter:

Emotional clutter:

Don't Worry about "Bad" Habits

The person who is dying gets to call the shots and make their own choices. I sometimes see family members denying their loved one things like cigarettes, alcohol, or foods they think are unhealthy. Let go of this impulse to control; these are not your decisions to make.

Are any of their personal choices making you uncomfortable? Work through your own feelings so that you can take a step back.

Don't Be Afraid of Pain Relief

It's not uncommon for a caregiver to feel nervous about administering pain medication, despite having a doctor's prescription. However, the decision to opt for prescribed pain relief is up to the patient, not the caregiver. Work through your feelings and concerns on this issue so that you can be the crew member your captain (loved one) needs you to be.

What concerns you most about administering prescribed pain medication when the patient requests it?

What fears, concerns, or beliefs does the use of morphine bring up for you?

How can you process these concerns, or put them aside for now?

Don't Shy Away from Discussing Death

I know this can be hard, but when your loved one brings up the topic of death, you do them a disservice if you dismiss it rather than acknowledging their truth. They know they're dying, and they deserve the space to talk about it.

What feelings come up for you when your loved one brings up the topic? How can you work through these obstacles to be more present instead?

Think about the knee-jerk reactions you may have when the topic of death comes up. What can you say instead?

I'M TEMPTED TO SAY	WHAT I COULD SAY INSTEAD
"Don't say stuff like that, Dad. You're not going to die."	"I love you, Dad. Is there anything I can do to help you feel more prepared?"

Don't Do It All on Your Own

One of the best ways to help your loved one is to ensure that *you* have all the help you need. This assistance can take different forms:

- **Accept help from people who offer it.** Who has reached out and in what capacity?

- **Ask for help from people who care.** Whom can you turn to, even if you don't know what help they could offer? Reach out, and ask to come up with ideas together.

- **Ask others to visit.** People resist visiting for a variety of reasons. Who would stop by if you asked them to? What holds you back from requesting visits?

- **Receive respite care offered through hospice.** Find out what options are available through your hospice provider. It might take some planning, but it would offer you a break.

- **Pay for help if you're able.** Not everyone can afford to pay for someone to assist with their loved one's care, but consider this possibility if you can. Others might contribute to the cost as well. Who might be able to help?

Additional notes and reflections

Evaluating Your Loved One's Decline

Caregiving is a big job, and part of the challenge is navigating changing family roles, particularly as an individual loses their ability to be independent.

Ask yourself, "Is my loved one able to remain **clean, safe, and comfortable**?" As I discuss in chapters 4 and 8 of *Nothing to Fear*, there are six basic areas to pay attention to, which health-care professionals refer to as the activities of daily living (ADLs):

1. Walking or functional mobility

2. Feeding

3. Dressing

4. Personal hygiene, such as bathing, grooming, and brushing teeth

5. Continence, or the ability to control bladder and bowel function

6. Toileting, or the ability to get safely to and from the restroom, use it, and clean oneself properly

For each of the above ADLs, is your loved one able to remain **clean, safe, and comfortable** while executing the activity? Make notes here, and continue to monitor these over time.

Walking or functional mobility:

Feeding:

Dressing:

Personal hygiene:

Continence:

Toileting:

Additional notes and reflections

Deathbed Phenomena

In my first book, *Nothing to Fear*, I describe some of the most common experiences that can precede death. Although unexplained, these phenomena prove over and over again that *death can be peaceful*. They show that our loved ones aren't suffering as they die. On the contrary, many of them are having beautiful visions, meeting with long-dead loved ones, or having spiritual experiences in line with their deeply held beliefs.

If you witness any of these phenomena, don't be alarmed. Be as present for your loved one as possible, and use the space on the pages that follow to collect your observations and reflections so that you can begin to process what's unfolding.

Visioning

"Visioning," also known as "deathbed visions," is when a person who is dying begins to see people or things that aren't physically present in the room. If a dying person experiences visioning, it usually begins somewhere around three or four weeks before their death. They may interact with these visions or simply perceive them. These visions are almost always calming in nature, preparing the individual for the journey to come.

If your loved one is experiencing visioning, what are you noticing? What emotions, memories, and reflections does it bring up for you?

Additional notes and reflections

The Death Stare

Closely related to visioning is another phenomenon that is more physically visible to those in the room with the dying person. It's called the "death stare" or the "death reach." About one or two weeks before death, a dying person will sometimes begin to look past everyone, staring at the wall, the ceiling, the corner of the room, or far off in the distance. They often won't look away from that point for a long time. This staring is often accompanied by the person lifting their arms, reaching out to something or someone.

If your loved one is showing signs of the death stare or death reach, what are you observing? How can you be present for them during this intense and emotional phase of the dying process?

Reports from the Other Side

Those of us who accompany someone during their journey through the process of dying often are privileged to hear their eyewitness reports of someplace "else." I don't know if these experiences prove there's an afterlife, but I do think they prove that death can be beautiful and is not something to be feared.

If your loved one is describing experiences from the other side, what are they saying? What does this evoke in you, and how can you be present for this remarkable moment in their journey?

The Rally

This phenomenon, known as the "rally," happens in about 30 percent of dying patients. It also can be referred to as the "surge," and the technical language for it is "terminal lucidity." I like to think of it as a patient's last hurrah. When it happens, we see a person who's been declining experience a burst of uncharacteristic energy. The rally can last anywhere from a few minutes to a few hours to a few days. They may look better, get up and walk around, talk to their family or caregivers, or eat a meal.

This period is marked by mental alertness that may not have been present in the weeks or even months beforehand. Even in patients who have been affected by degenerative diseases, a return of cognitive functions can happen for a short time. Family members might remark, "He seems like his old self again."

If your loved one is showing signs of a rally, what stands out to you most about their demeanor, their personality, and their energy level? What emotions does it bring up for you? Describe your feelings here, so that you can revisit and process them at a later time.

Additional notes and reflections

Choosing When to Die

Some dying patients seem to time their passing—either to co-incide with the presence of loved ones, the departure of loved ones, or a particular milestone of significance. This isn't some-thing we can control or something to feel guilty about if the tim-ing is not what we ourselves envisioned. I think of it as *what the person needed*. That doesn't mean it doesn't affect us as caregivers.

How does giving up control of your loved one's death feel for you? What emotions come up? How can you begin to under-stand the timing, and how, if at all, it reflects their needs and wishes? Use this space to begin to gather your thoughts.

Additional notes and reflections

Can Your Loved One Hear You?

We don't know for sure, but it's entirely possible that your loved one can hear you, even when they can no longer respond. Behave as if they can hear everything.

What do you want them to know? What would you like to tell them, even without receiving any acknowledgment from them in response? List some ideas here, and share your thoughts with them. Now is the time.

Additional notes and reflections

A Special Note to Caregivers: Just Be

I encourage you to pause from your *doing* and focus on just *being*. Be with yourself. Notice what's going on inside you. Capture some of your inner observations and feelings here—and continue in your own journal as needed.

Additional notes and reflections

What are the biggest obstacles, both practical and emotional, that you're facing as a caregiver?

Additional notes and reflections

How can you take steps to ease these pain points? Who else can you turn to? What ideas can you try to implement?

Remember, your baseline should be to ensure your loved one is **clean, safe, and comfortable.** Where are you succeeding most? Which parts are the most challenging?

Use this space to collect moments and emotions you'll want to look back on later as you reflect on this challenging, complex, and meaningful journey. What do you want to take with you? How have you grown or changed through this experience?

What emotions are surprising you most? It's not uncommon to feel shame, anger, or frustration with the person who is dying—or relief when thinking about their death, followed by shame and guilt. No feelings are invalid, and it helps to face them head on.

Anticipatory Grief (for Caregivers)

When we can anticipate the imminent death of a loved one, our grieving process likely begins while they're still alive. For example, when a person we love has dementia, we might feel a loss each time we observe another decline. This can be a profound and complex experience. Processing these feelings takes time and can be helped by working with a professional.

When you think about the profound loss of your loved one, what thoughts and feelings come up most? Use the space below to record and reflect.

Can you think of a time you felt grief during your loved one's dying process? Maybe each time they were hospitalized or a similar milestone you were hoping they wouldn't reach?

Grieving Together

In addition to processing your own anticipatory grief as a caregiver, you can be instrumental in helping the person who is dying process their own grief.

One way to do this is by expressing your emotions. What are you holding back that you could share with your loved one who is dying?

Another way of grieving together is by validating your loved one's feelings. As uncomfortable as it is, try not to minimize or deny what they're going through. How can you let the person who's dying express their feelings? What emotions does this bring up for you?

Self-Care for Caregivers

As you move through the caregiving and grief process, I urge you to be kind to yourself. Allow your emotions to surface, and give yourself time to heal. Here are some tried-and-true self-care methods, based on recommendations from grief experts:

Allow time for solitude. Although community is important to the grieving process, it's also essential to create moments of alone time for introspection and reflection. Giving yourself time to process emotions, memories, and the impact of loss can aid the healing process.

Practice mindfulness. Mindfulness techniques like simple meditation or breathing exercises can help you stay present with your emotions, acknowledge your grief without judgment, and cultivate a sense of inner calm.

Engage in physical activities. Taking walks, doing yoga, or participating in some other form of exercise can provide a change of scenery, help you feel present in your body, and release endorphins, which act as natural mood lifters and stress reducers.

Journal. Keeping a grief journal or otherwise expressing yourself through writing allows you to process your feelings, gain insight into your emotions, and find a sense of release and relief.

From the list on the previous page, which self-care practices are the most helpful to you as you process the complex emotions of grief and loss? Which ones have you yet to try? What's holding you back?

Death Is Not an Emergency

When our loved one dies, it's natural for caregivers to feel an impulse to *respond*. We might feel a sense of urgency to do all the things we think we should do immediately—make the person look presentable, call the mortuary, contact the hospice agency, care for the family and friends in our home, notify other loved ones, and more. We might even feel a bit panicky.

Whether you're with your loved one when they die or you discover after the fact that they have died, there is nothing you have to do immediately. Simply notice that what has happened is sacred. Death is a natural part of life, and you have, in whatever way, participated in your loved one's journey toward this sacred moment. I want to give you the freedom, when your loved one dies, to pause and take a deep breath. Death is not an emergency.

Nothing about this needs to be chaotic. There's no rush. There's nothing *urgent* you need to do when your loved one dies. I encourage you to pause and pay attention to what's happening in you and around you. Notice the sense of stillness. Stop and be present in the moment. Observe what you feel and what you need. Take in the silence, or turn on music if you prefer.

At some point, you'll make the call for the body to be removed from the home. Eventually, you'll phone everyone who needs to know. One day, you'll wash the sheets and make the bed. Ultimately, you'll handle the other responsibilities, too.

But when the person you love dies, there's nothing that needs to be done immediately. Death is not an emergency. Give yourself the gift of pausing to be present.

Part 4

Practical Considerations

*When patients have all the information
about their condition, they can make the
best choices about how to live more
freely and die how they choose.*

The pages that follow present some key information, suggestions, and reflection questions for anyone looking ahead to the end of life. I encourage you to start considering and planning early. Discuss your questions with your health-care team, legal counsel, and trusted loved ones. Consider these pages a first step in the process.

Advance Care Planning

Advance care planning lets patients and their loved ones review their options and make decisions about medical care ahead of time, so that if an emergency arises, the patient's wishes are clear and loved ones don't have to make agonizing choices under difficult conditions.

Here are some of the most common life-extending measures used in hospitals, which you'll want to consider when advance care planning:

Hydration: As I discuss in chapter 4 of *Nothing to Fear*, intravenous (IV) fluid is given through the veins.

Nutrition: A nasogastric (NG) or nasoduodenal (ND) tube is a flexible tube inserted through the nose to deliver nutrition into the stomach or intestines, respectively. Total parenteral nutrition (TPN) delivers nutrition through the veins.

Medications: These include vasoconstrictors to keep a patient's blood pressure up or IV medications to help regulate the patient's heartbeat.

Ventilator: This machine assists the patient with breathing.

Extracorporeal membrane oxygenation (ECMO) machine: Also known as a "heart-lung machine," this device is used in critical-care situations to oxygenate blood outside the body. This allows the blood to bypass the heart and lungs so these organs can rest and heal.

Continuous renal replacement therapy (CRRT): This type of dialysis machine is used twenty-four hours a day to slowly and continuously clean out waste products and fluid from the patient.

If you're dying, the decision about what life-saving measures you might want to receive is yours to make. I encourage you to speak with your doctor about which ones might be right for you. But as you're making decisions about what kind of medical care you want to receive, do consider your unique situation—what illness you have, how your illness is progressing, and if these measures truly will be beneficial. Think through the possible outcomes ahead of time, and consider situations in which you might choose to reject these measures.

On the pages that follow, collect your initial thoughts on these life-extending measures. What are your wishes, taking into consideration your unique health situation? I encourage you to think through these questions early, in consultation with your doctor.

My initial thoughts on . . .

Hydration:

Nutrition:

Medications:

Ventilator:

ECMO and CRRT:

Additional notes and reflections

Advance Care Documents

Two main kinds of legal documents are used to express a patient's advance care planning wishes in the United States: advance directives filled out by the patient and medical orders filled out by a physician. You can find more information on both these documents in my first book, *Nothing to Fear*. For the purposes of this journal, I encourage you to think through, in advance, the key decisions outlined by these documents so you'll be prepared to create them for yourself. And of course, be sure to discuss the actual documents with your legal counsel.

- **Power of attorney for health care:** Have you decided which person, such as a spouse, parent, or child, you'd like to designate to make medical decisions for you if you're unable to make them yourself? Use the space below to collect your thoughts on this question.

- **Health-care instructions:** These notes include whether you want life-extending measures, as described earlier, along with what kind of pain medication you want or don't want, and any other medical instructions you want to give. Collect your thoughts here as you consider these important questions.

- **Organ donation:** Most advance directive templates ask whether you would like your organs to be donated in the event of your death. Collect your initial thoughts here.

- **Primary physician:** Most advance directive templates let you list a specific doctor as your primary physician. Gather your thoughts on this question below.

What I Want at the End of My Life

In *Nothing to Fear*, I share a list of my personal wishes for the end of my life, if I end up needing hospice care. Of course, this list is not a legal or binding document, but I encourage you to come up with one for yourself, to share with family members as needed. Consider your age and health condition when answering, and keep in mind that your wishes might change as you get older or your health changes in the future. Topics could include the following:

Do I want IV fluids or a feeding tube at the end of my life?

Do I want to be intubated or administered CPR?

Do I want to be spoken to honestly, with the unvarnished truth, as if I'm fully present?

Is there a favorite TV show, movie, musical work, or other entertainment I would like played on a loop in my room? (This is basically about the "vibe" of your space.)

Ten Things to Do Before You Die

Here's a list to help you get started with some of the tasks that will make your death easier for your loved ones. If you have any questions as you consider these end-of-life decisions, ask your hospice social worker or the doctor you work with.

1. **Choose a mortuary.** It's useful to plan ahead on this, asking for recommendations from your support and care network. Use the space below to gather your notes and thoughts.

2. **Share your passwords.** Something as simple as creating a password list to give to a loved one can be a huge help after you're gone. Use the space below to gather ideas on which passwords to include and which trusted loved one to share them with.

3. **Draft a will.** I can't stress enough how important this is. If you haven't already begun this process, I encourage you to contact an attorney who specializes in estate planning. Use the space below to collect your notes and thoughts.

4. **Get your financial affairs in order.** If you don't have a financial adviser and/or estate-planning lawyer, consider finding one now so you can handle as much of your financial business as possible. Use the space below to gather notes. If you haven't started, what gets in your way most?

5. **Execute an advance directive.** As outlined earlier in this part, this is a legally binding document indicating which medical treatments you do and do not want. If you haven't already created one, use the space below to begin to gather your thoughts. What, if anything, is holding you back?

6. **Appoint someone to be your financial power of attorney.** This is someone who can sign a check in your name, sign your tax returns, and even buy and sell property that belongs to you. If you don't already have someone in mind, what's holding you back? Gather your thoughts below.

7. **Appoint someone to be your medical power of attorney.** This is someone who can make health-care decisions for you when you're no longer able to make them yourself. If you don't already have someone in mind, collect your thoughts below. What's holding you back?

8. **Consider how you'd like your body to be treated.** Do you want to be buried or cremated? If the latter, do you want your remains to be kept or scattered? Discuss your wishes with your loved ones, and use the space below to process your thoughts.

9. **Consider how you'd like your obituary to read.**
   This task is optional, but I encourage you to think about it and then share your wishes with a loved one. Is there anything specific you want included or left out? Any special language? Use the space below to gather your thoughts.

10. **Consider how you'd like to be memorialized.**
    This task is also optional, but many people find
    it meaningful. Do you want to be honored at a
    funeral service? A memorial service? Do you want
    to participate in a celebration of life while you're
    still living? Use the space below to envision your
    ideal gathering and then share your thoughts with
    a loved one.

Questions to Ask before
Signing Up for Hospice

In *Nothing to Fear*, and in my social media posts, I explain what hospice is and what it isn't. In short, hospice lets a dying person live their remaining days as well as they possibly can and then die as well as they possibly can.

Here are a few questions to ask hospice companies before signing up, along with the answers you ideally want to hear:

Q: How many patients does each nurse have on their caseload?

A: Twelve to fifteen (usually). If it's greater than fifteen, the nurse may have too many patients to care for them all effectively.

Q: What methods do you use to manage pain?

A: Examples include oral medications, liquid medications, continuous ambulatory delivery device (CADD) pumps, and pain patches.

Q: What kinds of care do you offer if symptoms can't be managed?

A: Continuous-care nursing or inpatient hospice care.

Remember, if you're dissatisfied with the care your hospice company is providing, you can always switch to another one.

The Comfort Kit

One of the resources we provide to people on hospice is a comfort kit containing several medications, including morphine or another opioid, antianxiety medication, antiemetics for nausea, bronchodilators, and over-the-counter pain and constipation relievers. A person doesn't have to use them if they're not needed, but they're readily available in case of emergency. This can be incredibly useful when your hospice nurse isn't present—for example, in the middle of the night—or when a regular pain reliever isn't working for some reason. As always, consult your hospice team with any questions or concerns.

Here's what's in the comfort kit (may vary slightly from hospice to hospice):

1. Morphine, used for pain and shortness of breath

2. Lorazepam, used for anxiety, agitation, and restlessness

3. Hyoscyamine, used to dry excess secretions that cause the "death rattle" (a wet rasping or gurgling sound with every breath, caused by saliva buildup in the mouth)

4. Zofran, used for nausea and vomiting, if needed (although most people don't have nausea and vomiting at the end of life)

5. Tylenol suppository, used for end-of-life fevers

6. Bisacodyl suppository, used for constipation

7. Bisacodyl pill, used for constipation

8. Haldol, used for agitation

Note that because it can be difficult for patients to swallow at the end of life, we don't use pills or liquids that need to be swallowed. The meds in the comfort kit are almost all taken either rectally (as a suppository) or sublingually (absorbed through the gum tissue under the tongue, with no swallowing necessary).

Final Note

We die the way we lived. Be intentional about both. Let death into your life. Talk about it with your loved ones. Don't leave them guessing about how you want to die. Don't wait for a terminal diagnosis. Do it now. Your death will be better because of it—and so will your life.

Additional notes and reflections

About the Author

Julie McFadden, RN, has been a nurse, first in the ICU and then in hospice/palliative care, since 2008. Her TikTok channel, which educates viewers about death and hospice care, has more than one million followers, and her work has been featured in media outlets including *Newsweek*, *USA Today*, *The Atlantic*, *Business Insider*, *People*, and *BuzzFeed*. Her *New York Times* bestselling first book, *Nothing to Fear*, helps readers demystify death so they can live more fully. You can find her on TikTok, Instagram, YouTube, and Facebook at @HospiceNurseJulie. She lives in Los Angeles, California.

Also by
Julie McFadden, RN

@HospiceNurseJulie